This Book Belongs To:

_____

Once upon a time in the colorful meadow of Sparksville, there lived a ladybug named Luckie. Luckie was known for her vibrant red color and beautiful black spots that adorned her wings.

Every day, she would play with her two best friends, Chase the caterpillar, and Bella the butterfly.

One sunny morning, as Luckie was fluttering around, she felt something strange.

She looked down at her wings and gasped in horror-all her spots were gone!

Luckie's eyes sparkled with gratitude as her friends suggested.

So, the trio set off on an adventurous
journey through the city
which was bustling with humans and their
colorful tall buildings.

Luckie, Chase and Bella searched
high and low for the spots,
under flower pots, and tall rooftop buildings.

But Luckie's spots were
nowhere to be found.

As the sun dipped below the horizon, Luckie began to lose hope.

Finally, Luckie had a big smile on her face and she couldn't help but to laugh from the joke. In fact Bella and Chase fell on the ground with her laughing.
It was a magical moment of Luckie letting go of all her worries and having fun with her friends.

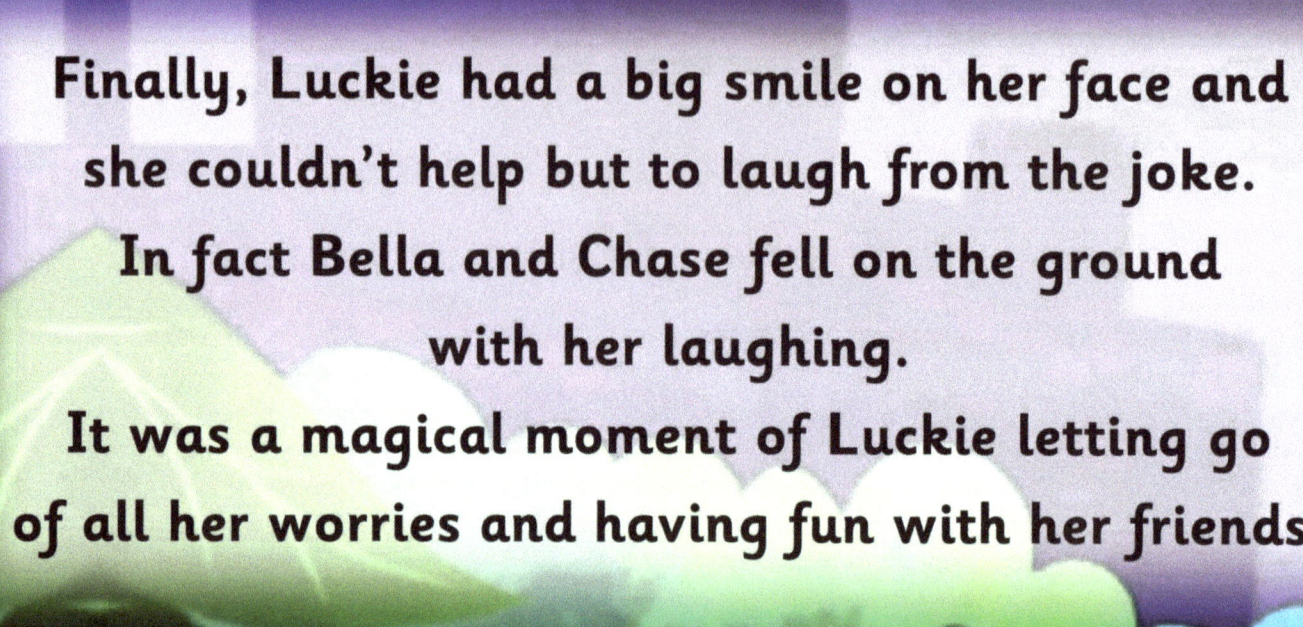

The next day, the friends continued their search, but still, no spots were found.

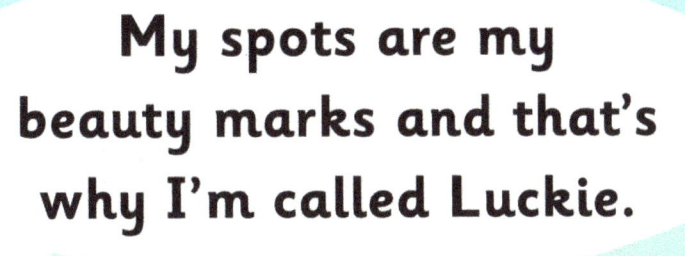

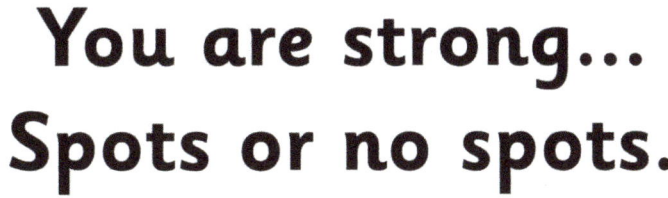

Feeling the love of her friends, Luckie wiped away her tears and took a deep breath.

She realized that her spots were just a small part of who she was.

She had so much more to offer and she didn't need her spots to prove her worth.

With a newfound confidence, Luckie decided to let go of her fear and worry.

You know what Chase and Bella?
You're right!
I'm more than my spots.
I am beautiful inside and out.
Not only am I a great ladybug
who has great friends,
but I'm a great friend too!
I believe in myself even
if that means not having
my spots!

And then, something magical happened, as Luckie embraced her true self and believed in her worth, her spots began to reappear but something was different, something felt different.

They were shiny gold spots one, by one shimmering on her wings like tiny stars. They were the most beautiful spots she had ever seen.

From that day on, Luckie, Chase, and Bella continued their adventures together, cherishing each moment and celebrating the uniqueness of the friendship.

Whenever, Luckie looked at her gold spots, she remembered that believing in herself was the real magic that brought them back.

The trio of friends continued to spread laughter love, and courage wherever they went. For in their hearts, they knew that true friendship and self-belief were the most precious spots of all.

The End

Printed in the USA
CPSIA information can be obtained
at www.ICGtesting.com
LVHW070712041123
763055LV00011B/52